SO-AZU-632

DATE DUE

324.973
SMA

904006
Small, Cathleen.

Elections and voting

SEQUOYAH MIDDLE SCHOOL
DEKALB COUNTY, GA 30340-2702

799258 00000   01036A   0001

AMERICAN DEMOCRACY IN ACTION

Elections and Voting

Cathleen Small

LUCENT
PRESS

Published in 2019 by
Lucent Press, an Imprint of Greenhaven Publishing, LLC
353 3rd Avenue
Suite 255
New York, NY 10010

Copyright © 2019 Lucent Press, an Imprint of Greenhaven Publishing, LLC.

All rights reserved. No part of this book may be reproduced in any form
without permission in writing from the publisher, except by a reviewer.

Produced for Lucent by Calcium Creative Ltd
Designers: Clare Webber and Simon Borrough
Picture researcher: Rachel Blount
Editors: Sarah Eason and Jennifer Sanderson

Picture credits: Cover: Shutterstock: Derek Hatfield (top), Alexandru Nika (bottom). Inside:
Shutterstock: Blend Images: p. 7; Chrisdorney: p. 30; Rob Crandall: pp. 32, 40-41b; Bill
Dowling: p. 9; Drop of Light: p. 12; Evan El-Amin: p. 31; Hadrian: p. 43; Jstone: p. 44c; A Katz:
pp. 16-17; KelseyJ: pp. 5, 44t; LO Kin-hei: pp. 6; Alexandru Nika: p. 27; Susan Schmitz: p.
40t; Sirtravelalot: p. 44b; Joseph Sohm: p. 13, 22, 24; Welcomia: p. 28; Lisa F. Young: p. 36;
Wikimedia Commons: 1946 Richard Nixon congressional campaign: p. 11; Burke & Atwell,
Chicago (Photographer): p. 18; Howard Chandler Christy: p. 14; Executive Office of the
President of the United States: p. 38-39; Gage: p. 21; Yoichi Okamoto: p. 34.

Cataloging-in-Publication Data

Names: Small, Cathleen.
Title: Elections and voting / Cathleen Small.
Description: New York : Lucent Press, 2019. | Series: American democracy in action |
Includes glossary and index.
Identifiers: ISBN 9781534563995 (pbk.) | ISBN 9781534563971 (library bound)
Subjects: LCSH: Elections--United States--Juvenile literature. | Voting--United States--
Juvenile literature.
Classification: LCC JK1978.S63 2019 | DDC 324.973--dc23

Printed in the United States of America

CPSIA compliance information: Batch #BS18KL: For further information,
contact Greenhaven Publishing LLC, New York, New York, at 1-844-317-7404.

Please visit our website, www.greenhavenpublishing.com.
For a free color catalog of all our high-quality books,
call toll free 1-844-317-7404 or fax 1-844-317-7405.

Contents

CHAPTER 1

The Election System

Elections and voting are two of the cornerstones of what make up the democracy of the United States. The U.S. government is divided into three branches: the executive branch (which includes the president), the legislative branch (the House of Representatives and the Senate), and the judicial branch (the federal courts and the Supreme Court). Understanding how the first two branches work can provide insight into the importance of the election and voting system established in the United States.

Separation of Power

Having both an executive and a legislative branch of the government ensures a **separation of power**. The president cannot pass legislation on his own—it must be passed first in Congress. The president can make **executive orders**, but the orders must work within the existing laws. If the president wants to make or change a law, he must lobby Congress to initiate legislation to do so. Congress can also check the president's power by confirming or rejecting appointees whom the president selects to his cabinet, and by overriding presidential **vetoes** on legislation.

Passing Laws

Congress cannot easily pass laws without the president's approval. Typically, when a bill passes both chambers of Congress, it is sent to the president for his approval and signature. However, if the

IMMIGRATION POLICY AND CHECKS AND BALANCES

Sometimes, the judicial branch provides a check on presidential power. In his first few weeks in office, President Donald Trump issued an executive order banning citizens from 7 predominantly Muslim countries from entering the United States for a period of 90 days. He also banned all refugees from entering the country for at least 120 days. Federal courts refused to uphold the order, and Trump lost his bids in federal appeals courts to have the executive order upheld. However, in June 2017, the Supreme Court partially lifted the block on the order, allowing people from the affected countries who had relationships with American citizens to enter, while the rest of the people from those countries can remain under the ban. They upheld a revised version of the ban in December 2017.

president vetoes the bill, Congress can decide whether to attempt to override the veto and pass the law without the president's approval. To do so, both the House of Representatives and the Senate must pass the law with a two-thirds vote. This is not a common occurrence. According to the United States Senate, more than 90 percent of vetoed bills never become law.

This system means that neither branch of the government can have too much power. It preserves democracy and prevents the nation from becoming a **dictatorship** or an **oligarchy**.

MUSLIMS
Support Justice & Equality for All
◈ C
www.cair

In early 2017, it became difficult for people from certain Muslim countries to enter the United States due to an executive order issued by President Trump.

How Voting and Elections Give Citizens a Voice

The separation of powers between the executive and legislative branches of government means little to citizens without their input. In theory, without the voting and electoral system, a small group of individuals could take over the presidency and Congress, and run the government however it wanted. Giving citizens the right to vote prevents this from happening.

American citizens vote for the president and vice president in an indirect vote. Citizens vote for the presidential candidate of their choosing, but their vote goes to selecting a member of the **electoral college**. The electoral college will then vote for the majority candidate for that particular territory. Citizens also vote for members of Congress. For both the House of Representatives and the Senate, this is a direct, popular vote. Each voting citizen in a particular state or region casts their vote, and the official with the most votes wins.

Citizens generally vote to elect officials whose values match theirs, and whom they think will vote for the laws that are important to them. California is a good example of this. A great majority of

In 2008 and again in 2012, the majority of American voters chose Barack Obama to be president. In 2008, he made history as the first black president in U.S. history.

Californians, particularly in the large urban centers of the state, tend to favor **liberal** views. Thus, it is no surprise that citizens from these areas consistently elect liberal politicians from the Democratic Party. Both U.S. senators from California are Democrats, and thus Californians know that their senators will vote for policies typically favored by liberals. These include women's rights, social programs for the needy, and inclusive immigration policies. On the other side of the coin are states such as Texas, which tend to have citizens with **conservative** values. The elected representatives in Texas are generally Republicans, who tend to support traditionally conservative legislation: more restrictive immigration policies, pro-life legislation, and so on.

By voting for an elected official who shares their values, citizens can influence legislation. If they vote in a liberal, they can be confident that their elected official will vote for liberal legislation. The same is true if they vote in a conservative—they can generally be assured that their representative will support conservative legislation.

On a local and state level, citizens can also vote for laws, taxes, and policies that affect them on a more localized level. It is another way that the election and voting system helps give citizens a voice in their state and country. Depending on who you ask, voting is a right, a responsibility, and/or a privilege. For citizens of the United States, participating in the voting and election system is a way to ensure that each person's voice is heard.

Voting is a right and a privilege that U.S. citizens earn when they turn 18 years old.

CHAPTER 2

Types of Elections

In the United States, there are a number of different types of elections. Elections can take place at the federal, state, and local level.

Local Elections to Federal Elections

The lowest level of government elections is local elections. These are typically held to fill open city and county government seats. Elections are held for mayors, members of the local school board, county sheriffs, and other similar positions. Local elections are often held at the same time as larger elections, such as federal presidential elections or **midterm elections**. Like state elections, local elections are regulated by state **legislatures**.

At the state level, many official positions are filled by election. For example, the state governor and lieutenant governor are elected positions in all states, as are members of the state Senate and state **assembly**. In some states, judiciary positions such as state supreme-court judges are also elected. State elections are usually held at the same time as presidential or midterm elections, though they can also be held during off years—it is up to the state.

Federal elections are the highest level of elections in the United States. They are held for official positions at the highest levels of the federal government. Undoubtedly the best-known federal election is the election for the president and vice president, which occurs every four years on a specified day, as required in the Constitution. That day is currently the first Tuesday after November 1 in a presidential-election year.

SPECIAL ELECTIONS

While local, state, and federal elections are generally held at regular, predictable, scheduled intervals, sometimes, special elections are held. Often, these special elections occur when an elected official dies or resigns while in office. However, this is not the case for the president. If the president dies or resigns while in office, the vice president steps in and assumes the presidency.

Often, an elected official resigns to assume another position in the government. For example, after the 2016 presidential election, five members of Congress resigned to take other offices: several accepted positions in President Trump's Cabinet, and one resigned to become the Attorney General of California.

Special elections are not uncommon: In the 115 Congresses that have convened since 1789, there have been nearly 1,500 persons elected in special elections.

U.S. citizens are assigned polling places, where they can go to cast their ballot in a regular election or a special election.

Elections for members of the U.S. Congress also take place during the presidential election. However, midterm elections for members of Congress also take place in the even years between presidential elections. For example, the most recent presidential election took place in 2016, and members of Congress were elected, too. The next presidential election will be in 2020, but there will be elections for seats in Congress in 2018 and again in 2020.

State and local elections are direct elections—citizens of the state or locality vote for their candidate of choice, and the candidate with the most votes wins. However, presidential elections work differently—they are indirect elections. The president and vice president are elected together, as a team, but they are elected by votes cast by the electoral college. The president and vice president win the election when they gain at least 270 votes from the electoral college.

The actual vote of each citizen is tallied as part of the popular vote, but it does not determine the winner of the presidential election. It is possible for a presidential candidate to win the popular vote but lose the election because he or she did not earn 270 electoral college votes. This happened in the 2016 U.S. presidential election—and that was not the first time, either.

Congressional Elections

Congressional elections happen during presidential elections and also in midterm elections. They are held to fill seats in the two parts of Congress: the House of Representatives and the Senate.

Members of the House of Representatives hold office for two-year terms. There are 435 members in the House of Representatives, and they include representatives from every state. The number of representatives from each state depends on the state's population.

America needs new leadership now!

Elect

RICHARD M.

NIXON

WORLD WAR II VETERAN

YOUR CONGRESSMAN

Often—but not always—presidents are first elected to Congress before they run for president.

States with greater populations have more representatives, because each representative is elected by a constituency of a particular territory in the state. Densely populated states such as California have many congresspeople because there are so many people to represent. California actually has more congresspeople than any other state, with 53 elected to the House of Representatives. Seven less-densely populated states have only one representative in the House. Some of these states are small states geographically, including Delaware and Vermont. Several states are moderate in size, but simply do not have a large population: North Dakota, South Dakota, and Wyoming. Surprisingly, though, the states with only one representative also include the largest state geographically in the United States, as well as the fourth-largest state: Alaska and Montana. Both of these states are quite large (Alaska is nearly three times as big as the next largest state, Texas), but simply do not have much population density. Thus, they only require one elected official to represent them in the House.

NON-VOTING DELEGATES

The House of Representatives also includes six non-voting delegates from U.S. districts and territories, including Washington, D.C., American Samoa, Guam, the Northern Mariana Islands, Puerto Rico, and the U.S. Virgin Islands. Non-voting delegates cannot vote on proposed legislation in the full House, but they are allowed to vote in the Committee of the Whole. This is essentially a committee composed of all members of the House, including non-voting delegates. However, whether their vote counts in the Committee of the Whole is questionable. Various congresses in recent years have changed back and forth on a rule about whether a non-voting delegate's vote counts in the Committee of the Whole. It is a complex system that revolves around which political party has control of Congress and how the non-voting delegates' votes might affect voting outcomes in a particular Congress.

Non-voting delegates are also allowed to vote in specific congressional and conference committees in which they participate. They can also introduce legislation.

Most of these non-voting delegates are elected every two years, though the delegate from Puerto Rico, known as the resident commissioner, is elected every four years.

This meeting of delegates from the House of Representatives took place in Washington, D.C.

The United States Senate

The other branch of Congress is the United States Senate. Each state has its own state Senate, but the U.S. Senate is a federal body of elected officials. There are 100 U.S. senators, two from each state, regardless of the state's size or population density. The senators are elected for six-year terms. The 100 Senate seats are divided into three classes, with a class being reelected every two years. In other words, U.S. senators serve six-year terms, but the entire Senate does not turn over every six years. Instead, a third of the Senate is reelected every two years, so that there is a rolling turnover in the Senate.

HOW WELL DO YOU UNDERSTAND AMERICAN DEMOCRACY?

Indirect elections, such as those used for the U.S. presidency, are not common. Many have argued that the presidency should not rely on this type of election, because it can be easy to manipulate the makeup of the electoral college. For example, a candidate for president may win the election despite losing in the popular vote. Others argue that direct elections are prone to corruption, which is the reason why the electoral college was established in the first place. What are your thoughts? Describe a different system that would prevent corruption and ensure an elected official was truly the choice of the people.

Senators and congresspeople are elected directly in a voting method known as **first-past-the-post**, not by an electoral college.

13

CHAPTER 3

The Constitution

The United States voting and electoral system was originally laid out in the country's Constitution, though the Constitution has been amended several times. The first 10 amendments are known as the Bill of Rights.

The Original Constitution

The original Constitution was created in September 1787 and **ratified** nine months later, in June 1788. It took effect the following year, on March 4, 1789, and it officially replaced the Articles of Confederation, which were put in force in 1777.

The signing of the Constitution took place in 1787, though it was not ratified until the following year.

The Constitution started with seven articles. The first three covered the three branches of government that still exist in the United States (see pages 4–5). The next three articles established the rights and responsibilities of states with regard to the federal government. The final article set forth the process used to ratify the Constitution.

Elections and voting are covered in Article I, Section 2, of the original Constitution, which states, "The House of Representatives shall be composed of Members chosen every second Year by the People of the several States, and the Electors in each State shall have the Qualifications requisite for Electors of the most numerous Branch of the State Legislature." In other words, a qualified group of electors from each state elect the members of the House of Representatives. Section 3 of Article I specified that two senators would be chosen from each state by the legislature of that state. The Seventeenth Amendment later changed these terms to a popular election in each state.

Also in Article I, Section 2, the Constitution lays out the requirements for these elected officials: "No Person shall be a Representative who shall not have attained to the Age of twenty five Years, and been seven Years a Citizen of the United States, and who shall not, when elected, be an Inhabitant of that State in which he shall be chosen." This means that members of the House of Representatives must be at least 25 years old, must have been a U.S. citizen for at least 7 years, and must live in the state that they will be representing. Section 3 of Article I specifies that senators must be at least 30 years old, must have been a U.S. citizen for at least 9 years, and must inhabit the state they are representing.

The Constitution referred only to men because at that time, women could not hold elected office. Times may have changed, but the original wording remains—with the understanding that "he" is meant as a gender-neutral pronoun in this context.

TIE-BREAKER VOTES

The Senate is composed of 100 members. So, in theory, a tie can occur when the Senate votes on legislation, if the vote is an even 50-50 split. According to the original Constitution, the vice president of the United States is also the president of the Senate. Normally, the vice president does not get a vote in Senate legislation, but if there is a tie, the Constitution states that the vice president can step in and cast a vote to break the tie.

This happened in 2017 when the Senate was voting on whether to confirm President Donald Trump's nominee for Secretary of Education, Betsy DeVos. Her nomination was highly contentious—many people felt that DeVos did not possess the experience to hold the position and had concerns over her plans to change the public education system. Republicans held power in the Senate in 2017, and so many assumed Trump's pick, DeVos, would be confirmed. However, two Republican senators voted against the confirmation. This meant that the Senate was deadlocked in a tie. Vice President Mike Pence stepped in and voted to confirm DeVos, which broke the tie. This was the first time in Senate history that a vice president has ever had to break the tie in a confirmation vote.

Vice president Mike Pence (right) cast the tie-breaking vote that led to Betsy DeVos (left) being confirmed as the Secretary of Education under President Donald Trump (center).

The Amendments

So far, the amendments to the United States Constitution have dealt with various topics. Some of these amendments have made changes to the voting and election process within the United States. For example, the Twelfth Amendment established the electoral college system for electing the president and vice president. The Amendment states, "The Electors shall meet in their respective states and vote by ballot for President and Vice-President, one of whom, at least, shall not be an inhabitant of the same state with themselves; they shall name in their ballots the person voted for as President, and in distinct ballots the person voted for as Vice-President, and they shall make distinct lists of all persons voted for as President, and of all persons voted for as Vice-President, and of the number of votes for each, which lists they shall sign and certify, and transmit sealed to the seat of the government of the United States, directed to the President of the Senate ... The person having the greatest number of votes for President, shall be the President."

The electoral college establishes that the president and vice president are not elected by popular vote. Instead, a designated group of electors from each state votes for the president and vice president. Those electors are chosen to represent the majority vote from each territory, though—so if a particular region in a state votes heavily for the Democratic candidate, for example, then the elector for that region will cast a vote for the Democratic candidate.

The Seventeenth Amendment, ratified in 1913, changed how senators were elected. Previously, senators had been chosen by the state legislature, but the Seventeenth Amendment stated, "The Senate of the United States shall be composed of two Senators from each State, elected by the people thereof, for six years."

Who Voted?

For a long time, only white male citizens could vote. That began to change when the Fifteenth Amendment was ratified in 1870. The Amendment stated that people could not be denied the right

Women staged the **Suffrage Movement** to fight for their right to vote in U.S. elections.

to vote based on their race, or if they had previously been slaves or **indentured servants**.

Although former slaves and men of other races were given the right to vote in 1870, it took a lot longer for women to be given the right to vote. Thanks to the Suffrage Movement, the states ratified the Nineteenth Amendment in 1920. It says, "The right of citizens of the United States to vote shall not be denied or abridged by the United States or by any State on account of sex."

It might seem that after the passage of the Nineteenth Amendment everyone had the right to vote, but this was not entirely the case. Citizens who could not afford to pay poll taxes or other related fees or taxes were denied the right to vote. In this way, governments ensured that many black people and poor white people were denied the right to vote—people from these **marginalized** groups generally could not afford to pay the poll tax, and so they could not vote.

The ratification of the Twenty-Fourth Amendment in 1964 changed that. It stated, "The right of citizens of the United States to vote in any primary or other election for President or Vice President, for electors for President or Vice President, or for Senator or Representative in Congress, shall not be denied or abridged by the United States or any State by reason of failure to pay poll tax or other tax." Finally, the Twenty-Sixth Amendment, ratified in 1971, established the legal voting age as 18 years.

HOW WELL DO YOU UNDERSTAND AMERICAN DEMOCRACY?

Despite all of these refinements to the Constitution in the form of amendments, **voter suppression** reportedly still occurs. Do you think voter suppression can ever be fully eliminated? Why do you think this? What legislation would you pass to try to limit it as much as possible?

CHAPTER 4

The Electoral College

The offices of United States president and vice president are elected by indirect election. The mechanism used is the electoral college. Essentially, the voters in a state vote at a general election, and their votes determine how the members of the electoral college for their state will vote for the presidency.

The Breakdown of Electors

The state's population determines the number of electors for each state. So, for example, California has far more electors (a total of 55) in the electoral college than a less-populated state, such as Wyoming (which has 3). However, even states with a lower population are guaranteed at least three electoral votes, because the number of electors per state is equal to the total number of Senators and representatives in Congress. Each state has two Senators and at least one member of the House of Representatives, so that means that each state has at least three members in the electoral college.

The electors in a state are chosen in a two-part process. Before the general election, the political parties in the state choose slates of possible electors. Depending on the state, these slates of electors are either nominated at the state's party convention or chosen by vote by the party's central committee.

The potential electors are usually people who have been recognized for service and dedication to the particular political party. They might be elected officials at the state level, or

This map of the United States shows how the electoral college voted in the 2016 election.

state party leaders, or perhaps people who are personally or professionally affiliated with the party's presidential candidate. However, they cannot be senators or members of the House of Representatives, and they cannot hold an office of trust or profit in the government. At the end of this process—however it occurs—each presidential candidate has a slate of potential electors.

The second part of the process happens on election day. When the state's citizens vote for their presidential candidate of choice, they are actually voting for their elector. For example, if the majority of voters in a particular region vote for the Democratic candidate for president, they will essentially be electing a Democratic member to the electoral college.

In total, there are 538 electoral votes in the United States. A candidate must win 270 of those votes to win the presidency.

In general, all of a state's electoral votes go to the candidate who won the popular vote. For example, in the 2016 election, all of California's 55 electoral votes went to Hillary Clinton, since she won the popular vote in the state. However, two states are exceptions: Nebraska and Maine. In those two states, two electoral votes go to the winner of the popular vote, and the rest (three more in Nebraska and two more in Maine) go to the winner of the popular vote in each state's congressional districts.

Faithless Electors

Technically, the electors are expected to vote as their voters indicate. For example, Arizona is traditionally a Republican (or red) state. Thus, the citizens of Arizona generally vote for the Republican candidate for president. And so, their electors in the electoral college are expected to vote for the Republican candidate on their behalf.

John Kerry ran for president on the Democratic ticket in 2004.

However, sometimes electors vote against their population and they vote for another candidate. For example, in the 2004 presidential election, an elector in Minnesota voted for John Edwards rather than for Democratic candidate John Kerry, who Minnesotans in that district had backed. Edwards was Kerry's running mate. While it is possible that it was a mistake, it is also possible that the elector simply chose to vote for the person they wanted, rather than the candidate indicated by the people.

HOW WELL DO YOU UNDERSTAND AMERICAN DEMOCRACY?

The 29 states that have laws in place to punish faithless electors generally charge such persons with a misdemeanor and a small fine. However the U.S. Circuit Court of Appeals has suggested that such laws may actually be **unconstitutional** and a violation of the Twelfth Amendment, which set forth how the electoral college would function in the United States. What are your thoughts? Should states be allowed to punish faithless electors? If so, what do you think would be a suitable punishment? Is a misdemeanor charge and fine fair or strong enough?

When this situation happens, the elector is known as a faithless elector. It does not happen often—the federal archives suggest that in the history of the electoral college, it has happened only in about 1 percent of cases. But still, it can happen.

In 21 states, this offense would go unpunished, as there are no state laws that prevent it. There are no federal laws or constitutional provisions that require an elector to vote according to the results of the popular vote. However, 29 states have state laws about this.

It is worth noting, though, that reportedly there has never been an instance of faithless electors affecting the final result of a presidential election. Many people feel that the 2016 presidential election was unfair because Democratic nominee Hillary Clinton had approximately 3 million more popular votes than winner Donald Trump, yet Trump won the presidency because he won the electoral college. While it is true that Clinton won the popular vote but lost the election because of the electoral college, it was not because of faithless electors. More likely, gerrymandering (see page 25) played a part, and there are allegations that Russian hacking may have influenced the ultimate outcome. In the end, Trump ended up with 304 electoral votes, far surpassing the required 270. There were reportedly a total of seven faithless electors: five who had been pledged to vote for Clinton, and two who had been pledged to vote for Trump. Even if those faithless electors had voted as their territory had supported, Trump still would have won the electoral college.

Although Hillary Clinton won the popular vote in the 2016 election, she still lost the electoral college vote.

GERRYMANDERING

Electors are chosen when the voters in a particular district vote for a particular candidate. For example, if in a given district 70 percent of voters voted for the Democratic candidate for president, then the elector for that district would be a Democrat expected to cast an electoral vote for the Democratic candidate. However, district boundaries can be manipulated so that the voter makeup of that particular district is altered. This is known as gerrymandering. If the boundaries for the example district were changed, that 70 percent of Democratic voters could flip to a Republican majority. Then the elector would be a Republican who would cast a vote for the Republican candidate.

Gerrymandering can be used to either help or hinder a particular political party. It can be used to pack an opposing party's voting power in one district so that it loses all the other districts, or it can be used to dilute the opposing party's votes across several districts.

There is nothing illegal about gerrymandering, though many consider it unethical. It happens often though, especially when certain regions have a high population of minorities. California has been accused of gerrymandering in several instances, in part because the Senate districts appear to have very odd boundaries. It is not entirely surprising, though. California's major cities tend to be heavily Democratic, but the lesser-populated areas tend to favor the Republicans. It is to either party's benefit to gerrymander in this case: Democrats would not want their electoral voting power diluted by getting only the districts around the major cities, and Republicans would want to enhance their electoral voting power by distributing the Democratic votes among smaller districts where they could be outnumbered by Republican votes.

CHAPTER 5

Popular and Electoral Votes

The United States is somewhat unique in its use of an indirect voting system for the offices of president and vice president. Some other countries also use indirect voting systems, such as Germany (for their presidential election) and India (whose president is elected by their parliament). However, it is not a very common election system, and many citizens prefer an election system determined by popular vote.

The Popular Vote

A direct popular election is simple: People vote for the candidate of their choosing, and the candidate with the most votes wins. This type of election system is widely used in the United States for many elections. At its simplest level, people use informal popular votes all the time. Family members might vote on what restaurant to visit for dinner. Friends might vote on what movie to see. Elementary school elections for class officers are generally decided by a popular vote. Popular votes happen every day, in countless ways.

Popular votes also happen often for state and local legislation. If a new tax or law is on the ballot, citizens can vote to approve or reject it. Federal laws, however, are voted on by members of Congress, so in a sense, they are decided by indirect vote: Citizens' elected officials are the ones casting the votes for or against those.

In the government, popular elections are also common. At the local, state, and federal levels, many officials are elected by popular vote.

While many elections are decided by popular vote, presidential elections in the United States are decided by electoral college votes.

Citizens vote for everything from school superintendents to state assembly members to representatives in the U.S. Congress. While this simple system works, there are instances when it does not. It is for this reason that the electoral college was established.

How the Popular Vote Can Fail

One danger of elections determined by popular vote is that they can become a popularity contest. If a candidate is charismatic and has the means to win over a large segment of the population, that candidate can, in theory, win a seat in office even if they are not really a good candidate. When the Founding Fathers created the electoral college, one of their goals was to prevent this from happening. They were afraid a strictly popular vote could result in a criminal or traitor ascending to the office of the presidency, and so they felt the electoral college would provide a kind of check-and-balance system on that.

The Founding Fathers felt that the indirect system provided the best possible way of ensuring that a qualified candidate would enter office. The people would have a voice because their votes would determine the electors who would make up the electoral college. The electoral college itself could carefully vet candidates to ensure that they were appropriate for the office of the president.

Providing Stability

In past history, democracies had been brought down by unfit leaders, and the Founding Fathers hoped that the voting system they developed would provide stability and prevent history from repeating itself. Largely, it has, and the United States has existed under this voting system for more than two centuries.

It was also hoped that the system would empower states. Under the system, citizens of states are unified in their voting as independent

It was hoped that the electoral college and voting system would help ensure that fit candidates for president would be elected to the office.

STRATEGY GONE AWRY?

Under the electoral college system, even sparsely populated states each have at least three votes, and thus wise presidential candidates will not ignore them. In fact, some feel this may be what brought down Hillary Clinton in her attempts to win the presidency in the 2016 election. She focused her campaign efforts heavily on the major cities in the United States, and citizens in the more rural or less-densely populated states felt that she was uninterested in their thoughts and wishes. Donald Trump made it a point to campaign in those very states, and he ended up winning them. In the end, those wins were enough to overtake Clinton, despite her having won the massive state of California, which is often the key to winning an election because it has 55 electoral votes.

entities are part of a collective whole. States are also empowered because those with large populations are prevented from getting all the attention during a presidential campaign. Under a popular vote system, a candidate would undoubtedly focus efforts on major centers, where they could appeal to the most voters in one place, ignoring places with fewer voters.

Abolishing the Electoral College

Trump's strategy of paying attention to the states Clinton was thought to be ignoring was a shrewd and profitable one, but some cite strategies like this as the reason why the electoral college should be abolished. They argue that candidates use this strategy to focus on **swing states**, to the detriment of voters in states known to vote steadily Republican or Democrat. If the electoral college were abolished, they say, then candidates would have to spread their focus and efforts more evenly.

HOW WELL DO YOU UNDERSTAND AMERICAN DEMOCRACY?

The Founding Fathers established the electoral college in part to prevent a popular vote from resulting in an unfit candidate taking office. President Donald Trump won the electoral vote in the 2016 election, despite losing the popular vote. However, many argue that he is unfit for the office of the president and lacks the basic knowledge a president needs to be able to effectively run the country. Hillary Clinton was not a particularly popular candidate either—many felt she was corrupt and questioned her fitness for the office. How well do you think the U.S. election system worked in the 2016 election? Do you think the electoral college resulted in the appropriate candidate being elected? Or do you think it failed and allowed an unfit candidate to assume office? What system would you put in place to try to ensure the fitness of a particular candidate for the office?

Others, such as analysts from the conservative Heritage Foundation, disagree and say that a national popular vote is a poor choice based on mistaken assumptions, because swing states can change from election to election and are notoriously unpredictable. Indiana, for example, was Republican for many years; then, in a surprise move, voted for the Democratic Party when Barack Obama was the Democratic presidential candidate.

Both Donald Trump and Hillary Clinton led fierce electoral campaigns in 2016, with Clinton winning the popular vote.

Those who support the electoral college also fear that switching to a national popular vote would result in candidates focusing their efforts on major population centers and once again ignoring rural or less-populated regions. But those who wish to abolish the electoral college cite gerrymandering and other methods of manipulating and influencing the makeup of the electoral college as reasons why a national popular vote would be a more appropriate way to elect the head officials in a democracy.

Abolishing the electoral college is unlikely to happen in the near future. It was put forth in the Constitution, which makes it very hard to change. Doing so requires a constitutional amendment, which the House and Senate have to approve by a two-thirds majority, and three-fourths of the 50 states must ratify it. In 2017, the Republican party had control of both the House and the Senate, and the Republican party is generally in favor of keeping the electoral college because it resulted in their candidate taking office. Even if Democrats regained control of the House and Senate after the next midterm election, they would face an uphill battle in trying to abolish the electoral college. Republican states make up the majority of the 50 states, and they tend to be in favor of the electoral college. And smaller swing states are generally also in favor of it because it gives them more of a voice than they typically have in a national popular vote.

Indiana, a traditionally Republican state, voted for Democratic candidate Barack Obama in 2008.

CHAPTER 6

Eligibility and Ways to Vote

Voting in the United States can be described as a right, a privilege, and a duty. Under the Constitution, eligible citizens have the right to vote in elections. Many consider it a privilege, too, because not all nations offer that right to their citizens. Others cite it as a civic duty—as a member of the United States citizenship, eligible voters have a duty to support their nation and their government by assessing candidates and legislation, and making an informed decision about how to cast their votes.

Voter Eligibility

The rules of voter eligibility in the United States were set forth in the Constitution and also in state laws. The rules have changed over time—gone are the days when women and nonwhite people could not vote. Now, the general rules about voting are as such:

U.S. citizens who are 18 years old have the right to vote as long as they have not been convicted of certain crimes and are not considered to be mentally incapacitated.

- Voters must be U.S. citizens.
- They must be at least 18 years old on or before election day.
- They must be registered to vote in their state (unless they live in North Dakota, which does not have voter registration).
- They must meet their state's residency requirements.

People who are prohibited from voting include:
- Those who are not citizens, even if they are permanent legal residents.
- Those residing in U.S. territories. This applies to the general presidential election. Citizens residing in U.S. territories have voting rights in other types of elections.
- Some people with felony convictions on their record. The laws vary by state.
- Some people who are considered to be mentally incapacitated. As with felons, the laws vary by state.

Although these are the general rules about who can and cannot vote, each state also has its own voting and election rules. State or local election offices can help citizens learn the specific voting and election rules for their particular state.

Voter Rights

While general rules about voting were established in the Constitution, several amendments (including the Fifteenth, Nineteenth, and Twenty-Sixth) to the Constitution further solidified the rules about voter eligibility and rights. The Fifteenth Amendment, ratified in 1870, sets forth that governments shall not be permitted to deny citizens the right to vote based on race, color, or past servitude (in other words, slavery or indentured servitude). The Nineteenth Amendment, ratified in 1920, was the result of the women's Suffrage Movement and granted women the right to vote. The Twenty-Sixth Amendment, ratified in 1971, lowered the voting age from 21 to 18.

In addition, the Twenty-Fourth Amendment, ratified in 1964, prohibited federal and state governments from requiring payment of a poll tax from those citizens wishing to vote. The poll tax had been adopted by Confederate states as a way to prevent former slaves, black people, and poor white citizens from voting. Much like gerrymandering, it was a smart attempt to manipulate election outcomes. If black people and poor people could not vote, their voices would not be heard. However, unlike gerrymandering, poll taxes were very clearly discriminatory, and thus the Twenty-Fourth Amendment was introduced and subsequently ratified.

The Twenty-Fourth Amendment outlawed poll taxes, which essentially gave black people and poor people the ability to vote.

NATIVE AMERICANS: A FORGOTTEN POPULATION

When thinking of historically **disenfranchised** populations in the United States, black citizens often come to mind. Their history as slaves, then being discriminated against by **Jim Crow laws**, and being at the center of the **Civil Rights Movement**, presents an ever-present reminder of their fight for equality in the United States. Even now, despite numerous protections under state and federal laws, black citizens struggle in some areas to achieve full equality in the United States.

However, there is another, smaller, often forgotten population in the United States: Native Americans. Of all of the many ethnicities that make up the melting pot of the United States, Native Americans may be the most often forgotten. Perhaps it is because many of them live on reservations, where tribal law sometimes supersedes state law, or maybe it is because some are so assimilated into the dominant white culture that they blend in with the greater population. But whatever the reason, the reality is that Native Americans are still very much a part of the fabric of U.S. culture, and their voting rights have been shaky throughout much of the country's history.

From the late 1700s through the 1800s, the U.S. government typically tried to keep Native Americans confined to reservations. They could live in the United States, but on reservations and by their own legal system. They were not technically recognized under U.S. law until the late 1800s, and even then they were not guaranteed U.S. citizenship, despite their tribes having been present in North America for hundreds or even thousands of years. They were not given citizenship, so they did not have the right to vote. In 1924, Native Americans were granted U.S. citizenship, but many states still restricted their voting rights by enacting property requirements, creating poll taxes, and even hiding the location of polls.

The Voting Rights Act of 1965 changed that. Native Americans were recognized as a racial minority and, as such, their voting rights were finally guaranteed and protected.

Although the Fifteenth Amendment prohibited governments from denying citizens the right to vote based on race, minorities still faced discrimination at the polls. The Voting Rights Act of 1965, which came out of the Civil Rights Movement, further protected the voting rights of racial minorities in the United States. For example, it disallowed the practice of requiring voters to pass a literacy test before they were allowed to vote. At this time, poor citizens and racial minorities often had low literacy levels, and so literacy tests were used to prevent people in these groups from voting.

How to Vote

There are several ways to vote in the United States. The first step is registering to vote, which is a simple process of filling out a voter registration form and submitting it to the local or state election office. The form is available on the Internet, or it is

Accessible voting machines exist for voters who have disabilities.

generally offered when a person obtains a driver's license. Often, as election day approaches, people from election offices stand outside supermarkets or other busy locations to allow unregistered people to register then and there.

The national election day in the United States is the Tuesday following the first Monday in November. However, state and local elections may be held other days, too. In any event, the state or local election office can direct voters to their polling place. Sometimes polling places change, so voters should always check with their state or local election office before heading to the polls.

Polling places are determined by address, so most voters' polling place will be near their home. Voters must go to their assigned polling place. However, if a voter must go to a polling place other than the place they were assigned, they may be able to cast a provisional ballot, depending on the rules in their state. The provisional ballot will be set aside and will not be counted until it has been determined for certain that the person is eligible to vote in the United States.

Voters with disabilities may have to request a change in polling place if their assigned polling place is not sufficiently accessible. They have to request the change before the election to ensure that they are included on the roster at the accessible location they have selected.

At some polling places, voters will be required to show an identification (ID) document to confirm their identity. This is subject to state laws, and states also determine what type of ID is considered valid. In many states, it must be a picture ID, such as a driver's license or passport. In other states, it can be a Social Security card, birth certificate, utility bill, or something similar. For voters who do not have any acceptable form of ID, many states will issue a voter ID card.

If a voter arrives at the polls and is unable to produce the appropriate ID document, some states will still allow the person to vote if they have a provisional ballot or with a signed form affirming their identity. States try very hard to allow as many people as possible to vote. This likely stems from the past in which disenfranchised groups were discouraged or outright banned from voting. This is a part of U.S. history that governments generally are not anxious to repeat, so voting is subject to state laws, but states will generally provide many ways for people to vote.

The Americans with Disabilities Act, signed into law by President George H. W. Bush, gave people with disabilities access to the voting system, and granted them other rights.

ACCESSIBILITY: LEVELING THE PLAYING FIELD

The United States has a history of not allowing certain groups to participate at the polls, so the government has revamped the system to ensure that as many people as possible can vote. Certain laws help people who might otherwise have difficulty voting. For example, the Americans with Disabilities Act (ADA) and the Help America Vote Act (HAVA) help people with disabilities and senior citizens preserve their right to vote. This ensures that people are given the opportunity to vote privately and independently, and have an accessible voting facility with voting machines designed for voters with disabilities. Accessible polling places have wheelchair-accessible voting booths, wide doorways that will accommodate wheelchairs, handrails on any stairs, and voting machines that can be used by blind or visually impaired voters. While voting is normally done independently and privately, voters with disabilities can bring someone to help them vote or can ask for assistance from those working at the polling place. The workers are not to influence the person's vote, but rather to help the person navigate the facility and equipment. While ballots are generally available in multiple languages, people who cannot read or write in any of the available languages can bring someone with them to read the ballot and help cast their vote.

Depending on the state or region, mobile polling places will sometimes be set up at nursing homes or long-term care facilities for residents who are unable to leave the facility. Organizations sometimes arrange for transportation to help people with disabilities travel to the polling place. And some polling locations offer curbside voting, in which a worker will bring the voting materials to the person's car. **Absentee voting** can also be an option for people who find it difficult to get to the polls for any reason.

Absentee Voting and Voting by Mail

People who are unable to travel to the polls can also vote by mail, using an absentee ballot. This can be useful for people with disabilities and elderly people, but it is also helpful for people who are temporarily away from home on election day, those who are serving in the military, and people who find it difficult to get away from their job to go the polls. Polling places have long hours, and many employers give their staff time off to vote, but it can still be difficult for some people to make it to the polls in person. The rules on who is eligible for absentee voting vary by state but, in general, it is not very difficult to get an absentee ballot. Each state has rules about what qualifies a person to receive an absentee ballot, but the requirements are often fairly broad. People wishing to obtain an absentee ballot can request one from their state or local election office.

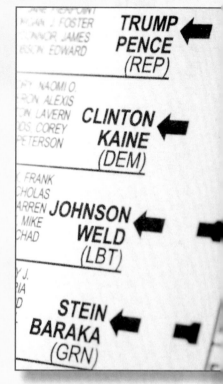

Ballots for presidential elections list candidates and their respective parties.

A few states do all their voting by mail. These include Oregon, Washington, and Colorado. All-mail voting means that all voters are mailed an official ballot that they can fill out and submit. However, they can also still vote at a polling place in person if they are not comfortable voting by mail. Every person is offered the chance to vote by mail, but that does not mean they have to do it that way.

Many states also offer an option for early voting. The dates and locations for polling places open for early voting vary, but generally, a state or local election office can help guide voters to the information they need to vote early.

Voting lines can be long at popular polling places!

HOW WELL DO YOU UNDERSTAND AMERICAN DEMOCRACY?

In the 2016 presidential election, there were reports of some groups being essentially blocked from voting because they did not have the right paperwork for identification. The state of Wisconsin changed its voter identification laws, which resulted in 9 percent of its registered voters lacking the appropriate identification needed to vote. A similar situation arose in Arizona and resulted in nearly 20,000 citizens being unable to vote. Lines at the polls were incredibly long because of the holdup with these voters, which caused others to turn away without voting. What would you do to try to prevent a situation like this from occurring again? Can you think of ways to ensure that voters are issued the correct identification before election day, or ways that the problem could be handled more efficiently on election day?

Elections and Voting

The United States election system is a complicated system with many branches. Yet at the same time, it is very accessible. State, local, and federal governments encourage U.S. citizens to have their voice heard by voting. They offer many opportunities for individuals to vote, and they make it a point to keep citizens informed of the candidates, laws, and taxes they will be able to vote on. Voter information booklets are often sent to registered voters before election day, so that they can become familiar with the candidates, laws, taxes, and other issues up for voting.

One tricky part of the system, though, is filtering out unreliable sources of information. When a person is up for election—whether a member of Congress, a local official, or the president and vice president of the United States—they will be heavily covered in the media. Some of the coverage will be factual and accurate, and useful for voters to understand. However, particularly in this age of social media and unchecked sources, there can be a lot of questionable material spread, and voters must be careful not to let biased or unsupported sources influence their voting. When Barack Obama ran for the presidency, one such baseless story that circulated was that he was not a U.S. citizen—that he had, in fact, been born in Kenya. Presidents must be natural-born citizens of the United States. Barack Obama was born in Hawaii and the stories of him being born in Kenya were false. But no matter how false they were, they were also damaging. Some people believe to this day that Barack Obama was not born a U.S. citizen, despite facts proving the contrary, and that may have cost him votes. He won the presidency in the long run, but that might not be true of every candidate—a candidate maligned in the press, even if the allegations turn out to be false, may not ever be able to fully recover.

President Trump is loved by some news sources and hated by others, so reports of his actions will vary based on which media outlet is covering them.

Whether the United States will remain a nation with both direct and indirect elections remains to be seen. There are certainly many who wish to switch the presidency to a popular vote rather than a vote by electoral college. Only time will tell whether the electoral college that the Founding Fathers established will stand in the future.

Regardless, the United States is a democracy in which voters have an opportunity to have their voice heard by casting a vote. The way to ensure that continues is by making sure as many people as possible get out to vote.

The Voting System in Action

Branch 1

Legislative makes laws

Branch 2

Executive carries out laws

Branch 3

Judicial evaluates laws

- Congress

- Senate: 100 elected senators, 2 senators per state

- House of Representatives: 435 elected representatives; representatives based on each state's population

- President

- Vice President

- Cabinet: Nominated by the president and must be approved by the Senate with at least 51 votes

- Supreme Court: 9 justices nominated by the president and must be approved by the Senate with at least 51 votes

- Other Federal Courts

Glossary

absentee voting Voting by mail in advance of an election, by a voter who cannot cast their vote at the polls.

assembly An elected group of people who make laws and decisions for a particular region or state.

Civil Rights Movement A social movement designed to end segregation and discrimination against black Americans.

conservative Describes one who values traditional systems and is cautious about new innovation.

dictatorship A country ruled by a person who has total power that was usually gained by force.

disenfranchised Deprived of a right or privilege.

electoral college The body of official voters, representing each state, who formally cast the votes for the president of the United States.

executive orders Orders issued by the president. These orders are not law, but if they are not challenged by the judicial branch of the government, they have the full force of the law.

first-past-the-post A type of vote in which the candidate who has the most votes wins.

indentured servants People who signed contracts requiring them to work for several years in exchange for gaining passage to the United States and for food, clothing, and shelter upon their arrival.

Jim Crow laws Laws that mandated segregation between black people and white people in the United States.

legislatures The lawmaking body of a state or country.

liberal Describes one who is open to new ideas and innovation, and is willing to change traditional systems.

marginalized Treated as insignificant.

midterm elections Elections held midway through a term of office.

oligarchy A country ruled by a small group of people.

ratified Given formal consent to a new law, treaty, contract, or agreement, thus making it valid.

separation of power The principle that power is divided among three branches of government: the executive, legislative, and judicial.

Suffrage Movement The fight for women to earn the right to vote and to run for public office.

swing states States that could be won by either Republican or Democratic presidential candidates.

unconstitutional Against what is stated in the constitution of a country.

vetoes Rejections of a proposed law.

voter suppression An attempt to influence an election by preventing or discouraging people from voting.

For More Information

Books

Freedman, Russell. *Because They Marched: The People's Campaign for Voting Rights That Changed America*. New York, NY: Holiday House, 2014.

Jack, Zachary Michael. *March of the Suffragettes: Rosalie Gardiner Jones and the March for Voting Rights*. San Francisco, CA: Zest Books, 2016.

Jacobs, Thomas A., and Natalie Jacobs. *Every Vote Matters: The Power of Your Voice, from Student Elections to the Supreme Court*. Golden Valley, MN: Free Spirit Publishing, 2016.

Lowery, Lynda Blackmon. *Turning 15 on the Road to Freedom: My Story of the 1965 Selma Voting Rights March*. New York, NY: Dial Books, 2015.

Websites

This United States website shows the three branches of government and explains more about how they function in relation to one another:
www.usa.gov/branches-of-government

The White House website has a short, but informative, page about voting and elections in the United States:
www.whitehouse.gov/1600/elections-and-voting

The United States government offers a website explaining the presidential election process in the United States:
www.usa.gov/election

This website from the University of Richmond's Digital Scholarship Lab offers maps and data on U.S. voting history from 1840 to 2008:
dsl.richmond.edu/voting

Publisher's note to educators and parents: Our editors have carefully reviewed these websites to ensure that they are suitable for students. Many websites change frequently, however, and we cannot guarantee that a site's future contents will continue to meet our high standards of quality and educational value. Be advised that students should be closely supervised whenever they access the Internet.